QUICK
& DELICIOUS

now you're cookin'

Colophon

© 2002 Rebo International b.v., Lisse, The Netherlands

This 3rd edition reprinted in 2006.

Original recipes and photos: © R&R Publishing Pty. Ltd.

Design and layout: Minkowsky Graphics, Enkhuizen, The Netherlands

Cover design: Minkowsky Graphics, Enkhuizen, The Netherlands

Translation and adaptation: American Pie, London, UK and Sunnyvale, California, USA

ISBN 13: 978-90-366-1479-5

ISBN 10: 90-366-1479-1

QUICK & DELICIOUS
now you're cookin'

THIS BOOK JUST MAKES YOU WANNA COOK

REBO
PUBLISHERS

Foreword

You have a busy lifestyle but also enjoy eating delicious food.
You eat out regularly but also like to cook at home. Sometimes you
take the extra time to cook. On days when you have less time on
your hands, this book offers you plenty of quick and delicious ideas.
It is full of contemporary dishes, generally from countries around the
Mediterranean, with lots of flavor but without the hassle.
Recipes include Lamb with Mint Butter and Mashed Potatoes and
Salmon with Pineapple Salsa, both of which you can make in no time
at all. There are plenty of healthy salads and nourishing soups, such
as Carrot Soup with Sweet Potatoes. Vegetarians are not forgotten
with Pumpkin with Lemon and Cheese or Herb Fritatta with
Asparagus and Ricotta. There are also lots of delicious desserts.
All these are perfect for special occasions too, when you want people
to think you went to a lot of trouble!

Abbreviations

tbsp = tablespoon

tsp = teaspoon

g = gram

kg = kilogram

fl oz = fluid ounce

lb = pound

oz = ounce

ml = milliliter

l = liter

°C = degree Celsius

°F = degree Fahrenheit

Where three measurements are given,

the first is the American cup measure.

Method

1. Brush bread slices with oil, place under a preheated hot broiler, and toast both sides until golden. Rub one side of toast with the cut side of garlic cloves.

2. For Tomato and Basil Topping, top half the toast slices with some tomato, onion, and basil, and broil for 1-2 minutes or until topping is warm.

3. For Eggplant and Feta Topping, brush eggplant (aubergine) slices with oil and cook under preheated hot broiler for 3-4 minutes each side or until lightly browned. Top remaining toasts with eggplant (aubergine) slices and sprinkle with feta cheese and black pepper to taste.

Cook under a preheated hot broiler for 1-2 minutes or until topping is warm.

Makes 16-20

Ingredients

1 French bread stick, cut into ½ in/1cm slices

2 tbsp/30ml olive oil

2 cloves of garlic, halved

Tomato and basil topping:

2 tomatoes, sliced

1 red onion, sliced

2 tbsp/50g shredded basil leaves

Bruschetta

Eggplant and feta topping:

2 baby eggplant (aubergines), sliced

1 tbsp/15ml olive oil

½ cup/4oz/125g feta cheese, crumbled

freshly ground black pepper

Method

1. Arrange the tomatoes, mozzarella, green onions (scallions), and olives in layers on serving dishes and season to taste.

2. To make the dressing, heat the oil and garlic in a small saucepan over a very low heat for 2 minutes or until the garlic has softened but not browned. Remove the pan from the heat, add the vinegar and basil, then pour over the salad.

Tomato and Mozzarella Salad

Ingredients

6 plum tomatoes, sliced

1 cup/8oz/250g mozzarella, drained and sliced

2 green onions (scallions), sliced

6 tbsp/90g black olives

salt and black pepper

Dressing:

3 tbsp/45ml extra-virgin olive oil

1 clove of garlic, crushed

2 tsp/10ml balsamic vinegar

2 tbsp/10g chopped fresh basil

Method

1. Melt butter in a saucepan over a medium heat. Add onion, carrots, and sweet potato. Cook for 5 minutes.

2. Stir in the broth and bring to the boil. Simmer for 30 minutes. Cool slightly.

3. Purée the soup in a blender, then pour it into a clean saucepan. Stir in the sour cream. Cook, without boiling, stirring constantly, for 5 minutes or until soup is hot. Stir in the dill. Serve immediately.

Ingredients

2 tbsp/1oz/30g butter

1 large onion, chopped

3 large carrots, chopped

1 large sweet potato, chopped

4 cups/1¾ pints/1 l chicken or vegetable stock

¾ cup/6fl oz/185ml sour cream

2 tbsp/50g chopped fresh dill

Carrot and Sweet Potato Soup

Method

1. Line a large serving platter or salad bowl with lettuce. Top with tomatoes, cucumber, red bell pepper, onion, feta cheese, and olives.

2. To make the dressing, put the oil, lemon juice, mint, and marjoram in a screwtop jar. Season to taste. Shake well. Spoon over salad. Serve immediately.

Greek Salad

Ingredients

1 lettuce, leaves separated and shredded

2 tomatoes, sliced

1 small cucumber, sliced

1 red bell pepper, cut into thin strips

1 small onion, thinly sliced

1 cup/8oz/250g feta cheese, cut into small cubes

12 black olives

Lemon and Mint Dressing:

6 tbsp/90ml olive oil

2 tbsp/30ml lemon juice

2 tsp/10g chopped fresh mint

2 tsp/10g chopped fresh marjoram

Method

1. Preheat the oven to 400°F/200°C. To make the croûtons, place the bread cubes on a cookie sheet and bake for 10-12 minutes, until crisp and golden, turning occasionally.

2. Preheat the broiler to high. Broil the prosciutto for 1 minute or until very crisp, then leave to cool for 2 minutes. Place the lettuce leaves, croûtons, and Parmesan in a bowl.

3. To make the dressing, put the anchovies, oil, mayonnaise, garlic, vinegar, Worcestershire sauce, and black pepper into a bowl and whisk until smooth. Spoon the mixture over the lettuce and croûtons, then toss until well coated. Top with the crispy prosciutto and extra Parmesan, if using.

Caesar Salad with Crispy Prosciutto

Ingredients

1in/2.5cm thick slices day-old bread, cut into ½in/1cm cubes

4 large slices prosciutto

2 cos or romaine lettuces, torn into bite-sized pieces

½ cup/4oz/125g parmesan, grated, plus extra to serve (optional)

Dressing:

8 anchovies, drained and mashed

2 tbsp/30ml extra-virgin olive oil

3 tbsp/45ml reduced-calorie mayonnaise

1 clove of garlic, crushed

1 tsp/5ml white wine vinegar

½ tsp/2.5ml Worcestershire sauce

black pepper

Method

1. Heat the oil in a frying pan over a medium heat, add the garlic, chickpeas, and rosemary and cook, stirring, for 5 minutes. Remove pan from heat and set aside to cool slightly.

2. Place chickpea mixture, sun-dried tomatoes, eggplant (aubergines), olives, feta cheese, and arugula (rocket) or watercress in a bowl and toss to combine. Sprinkle with olive oil and vinegar.

Serving suggestion: Serve with thick slices of fresh whole-wheat bread. Canned ratatouille can be used in place of the marinated eggplant (aubergines) if you wish.

ingredients

1 tbsp/15ml olive oil

2 cloves of garlic, crushed

2 x 14oz/440g canned chickpeas, drained

2 tbsp/10g chopped fresh rosemary

3oz/90g sun-dried tomatoes, sliced

½ cup/4oz/125g marinated eggplant (aubergine), sliced

Mediterranean Chickpea Salad

½ cup/4oz/125g pitted marinated olives

1 cup/8oz/250g feta cheese, crumbled

½ cup/4oz/125g arugula (rocket) or watercress

1 tbsp.15ml olive oil

3 tbsp/45ml balsamic or red wine vinegar

Method

1. Melt the butter in a saucepan and fry the potatoes, onion, garlic, ginger, and curry paste for 5 minutes, or until lightly golden.

2. Add the broth, coconut milk, lime juice, and chili pepper. Bring to the boil, cover, and simmer for 15 minutes or until the potatoes are tender.

3. Leave the soup to cool a little, then purée half of it using a hand-mixer. Return the purée to the pan, add the spinach, and cook for 1-2 minutes, or until the spinach has just wilted and the soup has heated through. Season to taste.

Coconut, Sweet Potato, and Spinach Soup

Ingredients

2 tbsp/1oz/25g butter

1 lb/450g sweet potatoes,

cut into ½ in/1cm dice

1 onion, chopped

2 cloves of garlic, crushed

1 tsp/5g grated fresh root ginger

1 tbsp/15ml medium curry paste

2½ cups/1 pint/600ml vegetable broth

1 cup/8fl oz/250ml coconut milk

juice of 1 lime

½ tsp/2.5g crushed dried chili peppers

3 cups/12oz/350g fresh spinach, shredded

salt and black pepper

Method

1. Heat oil in a wok over a medium heat, add leeks and bacon and stir-fry for 5 minutes or until bacon is crisp. Transfer leek mixture to a bowl, add parsley, basil, and oregano and mix to combine. Set aside.

2. In a bowl, combine the eggs, milk, cheese, and black pepper to taste and beat well. Pour one-quarter of the egg mixture into wok and swirl so mixture covers base and sides. Top with one-quarter of the leek mixture and cook for 1 minute or until set. Remove from wok, roll up, and place on a slice of toast. Repeat with remaining mixture to make 4 omelets.

Note: Fresh mint can be used in place of the oregano if you wish. For a vegetarian version, omit the bacon and replace with well-drained, cooked spinach. Squeeze as much moisture as possible from the spinach before making the omelet.

ingredients

2 tsp/10ml vegetable oil

2 leeks, chopped

6 slices bacon, chopped

2 tbsp/30g minced parsley

2 tbsp/30g chopped fresh basil

2 tbsp/30g chopped fresh oregano

6 eggs, lightly beaten

Bacon and Herb Omelet

½ cup/4fl oz/125ml milk

2oz/60g sharp yellow cheese, grated

freshly ground black pepper

4 thick slices whole-wheat or multigrain bread, toasted

Method

1. Preheat the broiler to high. In a bowl, combine the crème fraîche, horseradish, dill, lemon juice, and honey. Season to taste.

2. Toast the pikelets or muffins (first splitting the muffins) under the broiler for 1-2 minutes, until golden, then turn them over and cook for a further 1-2 minutes. Top each pikelet with a spoonful of the crème fraîche mixture, some smoked salmon, and a sprinkling of black pepper. Serve garnished with dill.

Crumpets or Muffins with Smoked Salmon and Horseradish

Ingredients

½ cup/4fl oz/125ml crème fraîche

1 tbsp/15ml creamed horseradish

1 tbsp/15g chopped fresh dill

2 tsp/10ml fresh lemon juice

½ tsp/2.5g clear honey

salt and black pepper

8 crumpets or English muffins

8oz/250g smoked salmon slices

Method

1. Using a sharp knife score around the circumference of each potato.

2. Place potatoes evenly around edge of microwave turntable and cook on HIGH (100%) for 5 minutes, turn over and cook for 3-5 minutes longer or until potatoes are done. Set aside until cool enough to handle, then remove skin, and cut potatoes into 1cm/½ in cubes.

3. Place onion and bacon in a microwave-proof bowl, cover and cook on HIGH (100%) for 3 minutes, stir, then cook for 2 minutes longer.

4. Stir in cornstarch, broth, and vinegar, cover and cook for 4 minutes. Add mustard, cream, and potatoes and mix gently to combine. Cover and cook on MEDIUM (50%) for 2 minutes or until hot. Season to taste with black pepper and sprinkle with chives. Serve warm.

Note: This is a good hot dish to serve at a salad buffet or barbecue. Flat oval-shaped potatoes seem to cook the most evenly in the microwave.

Hot Potato Salad

Ingredients

4 red-skinned potatoes, about 1½ lb/750g

1 onion, diced

2 slices lean bacon, chopped

2 tbsp/30g cornstarch

1 cup/8fl oz/250ml vegetable broth

¼ cup/2fl oz/60ml cider or tarragon vinegar

2 tbsp/30ml wholegrain mustard

⅓ cup/3fl oz/90ml heavy (double) cream

freshly ground black pepper

snipped fresh chives to garnish

Method

1. Heat oil in a saucepan over a medium heat, add onion, and cook, stirring, for 4-5 minutes or until onion is soft. Add chicken and cook for 2 minutes longer or until chicken just changes color.

2. Add potatoes and broth and bring to the boil. Reduce heat and simmer for 10 minutes or until potatoes are almost cooked. Stir the corn, milk, bayleaf, and black pepper to taste into broth mixture and bring to the boil. Reduce heat and simmer for 3-4 minutes or until potatoes are cooked. Discard bayleaf. Stir in lemon juice, parsley, chives, and black pepper to taste. Just prior to serving, sprinkle with Parmesan cheese.

Ingredients

1 tbsp/15ml vegetable oil

1 small onion, diced

8 oz/250g boneless chicken breast fillets, shredded

3 potatoes, chopped

3 cups/24 fl oz/750ml chicken broth

1½ cups/12oz/350g canned corn kernels, drained and chopped

1¼ cups/10 fl oz/300ml milk

Chicken and Corn Chowder

1 bayleaf

freshly ground black pepper

1 tbsp/15ml lemon juice

2 tbsp/50g chopped, fresh parsley

1 tbsp/15g snipped fresh chives

½ cup/8ox/250g grated Parmesan cheese

Method

1. Bring the chicken broth to the boil in a medium pot. Gradually beat in the cornmeal and cook over a medium heat for 8 minutes or until the cornmeal starts to come away from the side of the pot. Cover and keep warm.

2. Dust the veal escalopes in flour, shaking off any excess. Heat the olive oil and olive oil spread in a large, deep frying pan. Add the veal and cook over a medium heat until golden-brown on both sides. This will only take a couple of minutes on each side. Remove and keep warm.

3. Add the wine to the pan and bring to the boil, stirring to remove any juices that may be stuck to the bottom. Boil until reduced by half. Add the lemon zest, juice, and lima (broad) beans and boil until the sauce has reduced and thickened slightly. Return the veal to the pan and heat through. Stir in the capers and minced parsley.

4. Lightly spray the sage leaves with olive oil spray, broil until crisp, and scatter over the veal.

5. Drizzle vinegar over the tomatoes and season with pepper.

Serve the veal on the cornmeal mush with the tomatoes on the side.

Veal with Lemon, Crisp Sage, and Cornmeal Mush

Ingredients

2 cups/16 fl oz/500ml reduced salt chicken broth

1 cup/8 oz/250g instant yellow cornmeal

4 large veal escalopes (thin, boneless slices)

all-purpose (plain) flour, for dusting

2 tsp/10ml olive oil

4 tsp/20g olive oil spread

6 tbsp/3 fl oz/80ml dry white wine

1 lemon, rind grated, juice squeezed

1 cup/8oz/250g frozen lima (broad) beans, thawed and peeled

1 tbsp/15g baby capers

1 tbsp/15g minced parsley

12 fresh sage leaves

olive oil cooking spray

1 tbsp/15ml balsamic vinegar

3 beefsteak tomatoes, cut into thick slices

cracked black pepper to taste

Method

1. Place beef, bread crumbs, Parmesan cheese, oregano, minced garlic, eggs, and black pepper to taste in a bowl and mix to combine. Form mixture into sixteen balls.

2. Heat oil in a frying pan over a medium heat, add meatballs and cook, turning frequently, for 10 minutes or until brown on all sides. Remove meatballs from pan and set aside.

3. Add red bell pepper, onion, and garlic to same pan and cook, stirring, for 3 minutes. Add mushrooms and cook for 4 minutes longer. Stir in pasta sauce, return meatballs to pan, cover and bring to simmering. Simmer, stirring occasionally, for 10 minutes.

Serve spooned over hot spaghetti or other pasta of your choice.

Tip:

This dish can be made 1-2 days in advance and reheated in the microwave oven when required.

Ingredients

2 cups/1 lb/500g lean ground beef

½ cup/2oz/60g dry bread crumbs

2 tbsp/30g grated Parmesan cheese

1 tsp/5g dried oregano

½ tsp/2.5g garlic powder or 1 tsp/5ml garlic paste

2 eggs, beaten

freshly ground black pepper

1 tbsp/15ml olive oil

1 red bell pepper, diced

Italian Meatballs

1 onion, diced

3 large cloves of garlic, crushed

8 mushrooms, chopped

2 cups/16fl oz/500ml bottled tomato pasta sauce

Method

1. Heat the oil in a large, heavy-based saucepan or frying pan, then add the onion and fry for 3-4 minutes, until golden. Add the rice and stir for 1 minute or until coated with the oil. Stir in the wine and bring to the boil, then reduce the heat and continue stirring for 4-5 minutes, until the wine has been absorbed by the rice.

2. Pour about one-third of the broth into the rice and simmer for 4-5 minutes, until the broth has been absorbed, stirring constantly. Add half the remaining broth and cook, stirring, until absorbed. Add the remaining broth and the asparagus and cook, stirring, for 5 minutes or until the rice and asparagus are tender but still firm to the bite.

3. Add the butter and half the Parmesan and season. Cook for 1 minute, or until the butter and cheese have melted into the rice, stirring constantly. Sprinkle with the remaining Parmesan the parsley and lemon rind.

Asparagus and Lemon Risotto

Ingredients

2 tbsp/30ml olive oil

1 onion, chopped

2 cups/16oz/500g arborio (Italian short-grained) rice

1 cup/8fl oz/250ml dry white wine

3 cups/24fl oz/750ml chicken or vegetable broth

1 cup/8oz/250g asparagus tips, cut into bite-sized

pieces

4 tbsp/2oz/50g butter

½ cup/4oz/125g Parmesan, grated

salt and black pepper

2 tbsp/30g minced parsley

1 lemon, rind grated

Method

1. Preheat the broiler to high. Place the asparagus on the broiler pan and broil for 10 minutes or until charred and tender, turning once. Keep warm.

2. Meanwhile, beat together the eggs, garlic, herbs, and seasoning.

Melt 2 tbsp/1oz/25g of the butter in a cast iron frying pan until it starts to foam, then immediately pour in a quarter of the egg mixture and cook for 1-2 minutes, stirring occasionally, until almost set.

3. Place under the preheated broiler for 3-4 minutes, until the egg is cooked through and the top of the frittata is set, then transfer to a plate. Keep warm while you make the 3 remaining frittatas, adding more butter when necessary.

4. Arrange a quarter of the asparagus and 1 tbsp/15g of the ricotta over each frittata, sprinkle with the lemon juice, season, and drizzle with oil.

Top with shavings of Parmesan and garnish with fresh chives.

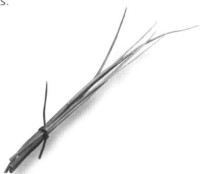

Asparagus, Ricotta, and Herb Frittata

Ingredients

1 lb/450g fresh asparagus

12 medium eggs

2 small cloves of garlic, crushed

4 tbsp/60g chopped fresh mixed herbs, to include

basil, chives and parsley

salt and black pepper

4 tbsp/2oz/50g butter

4 tbsp/60g ricotta

1 lemon, juice squeezed

olive oil or truffle oil to drizzle

Parmesan to serve

and fresh chives to garnish

Method

1. Place flour, ½ tsp/2.5g oregano and black pepper to taste in a shallow dish and mix to combine. Place egg, water, and black pepper to taste in a separate shallow dish and whisk to combine. Place bread crumbs and remaining oregano in a third shallow dish and mix to combine.

2. Place the pork schnitzels between two sheets plastic wrap and beat them with a steak hammer to make them thinner.

3. Coat pork with flour mixture, then dip in egg mixture, and finally coat with bread crumb mixture. Line a plate with plastic wrap, and place the coated pork scallops on it. Chill for 10-15 minutes.

4. Heat 2-3 tbsp oil in a frying pan over a medium-high heat and cook 1-2 schnitzels (escalopes) at a time for 3 minutes each side. Remove from pan, set aside, and keep warm.

5. To make the sauce, melt the butter in same pan, then stir in lemon juice. Spoon sauce over meat and serve immediately.

Tip:

When cooking the meat it is important not to crowd the pan or the meat will steam, rather than fry, and the coating will be soggy. Lean veal or turkey breast can be substituted for the pork.

Ingredients

all-purpose flour for coating

1 tsp/5g dried oregano

freshly ground black pepper

1 egg, beaten

1 tbsp cold water

dried bread crumbs

8 pork schnitzels (escalopes)

(about 6oz/175g each)

vegetable oil

Lemon butter sauce:

2 tsp/10g butter

1 tbsp/15ml lemon juice

Vienna Schnitzel in Lemon Sauce

Method

1. Combine the vinegar, honey, garlic, Chinese spices, salt, and pepper in a bowl. Cut several slashes in each duck breast with a sharp knife and rub in the mixture. Set aside.

2. Rinse the grated potatoes, squeeze dry in a clean kitchen towel, then season. Heat ½ oz/15g butter and 1 tbsp/15ml of the oil in a frying pan, add 4 tbsp/60g of the mixture (about half) and press down gently to make 4 röstis. Fry for 5-6 minutes on each side, until browned and cooked through. Repeat to make 4 more.

3. Meanwhile, preheat the broiler to high. Broil the duck close to the heat for 3-4 minutes on each side, until charred. Wrap in foil and leave to rest for 5 minutes, then slice, and serve with the pan juices, the röstis, and a little chutney. Garnish with the fresh herbs.

Balsamic Duck Breasts with Potato Röstis

Ingredients

2 tbsp/30ml balsamic vinegar	1 lb/450g waxy potatoes, peeled and grated
1 tsp/5ml clear honey	2 tbsp/30g butter
1 clove of garlic, crushed	2 tbsp/30ml olive oil
pinch of Chinese five-spice powder	4 tbsp/60g apple and plum chutney
salt and black pepper	to serve: fresh herbs, such as marjoram
4 boneless duck breasts, about 6 oz (175g) each	or basil, to garnish

Method

1. Combine olive and vegetable oils together in a large saucepan over a low heat, add onions and cook, stirring frequently, for 10 minutes or until onions are golden. Remove from pan and set aside.

2. Increase heat to high and cook lamb in batches for 4-5 minutes or until lamb is well browned. Remove lamb from pan and set aside.

3. Wash rice under cold running water until water runs clear. Drain well. Add rice to pan and cook, stirring constantly, for 5 minutes. Slowly stir boiling broth into pan. Add thyme, oregano, and black pepper to taste, then reduce heat, cover pan with a tight-fitting lid, and simmer for 20 minutes or until all liquid is absorbed. Return lamb and onions to pan, cover and cook for 5 minutes longer.

4. Remove pan from heat and using a fork to fluff up rice mixture. Sprinkle with raisins and almonds and serve.

Note: When cooking pilau, it is important that the lid fits tightly on the pan. If the lid does not fit the pan tightly, first cover with aluminum foil, then with the lid.

Ingredients

2 tbsp/30ml olive oil

2 tbsp/30ml vegetable oil

3 onions, quartered

1 lb/500g lean diced lamb

1 scant cup/7oz/220g long-grain rice

3 cups/24 fl oz/750ml boiling chicken or beef broth

1 tsp/5g dried thyme

Lamb and Almond Pilau

1 tsp/5g dried oregano

freshly ground black pepper

½ cup/4oz/125g raisins

4 tbsp/2oz/50g whole almonds, toasted

Method

1. Preheat the oven to 400°F/200°C. Cut a deep slice into one side of each chicken breast to make a pocket. Place 2 sun-dried tomatoes in each pocket, then wrap 2 bacon slices around each breast. Secure with wetted cocktail sticks.

2. Heat 1 tbsp/15ml of the oil in an ovenproof frying pan. Cook the chicken for 2-3 minutes, turning once, until browned all over. Transfer to the oven and cook for 15 minutes or until the chicken is cooked through. Transfer to a plate, remove the cocktail sticks, and keep warm. Meanwhile, preheat the broiler to high. Brush the leeks with the remaining oil and broil for 6-8 minutes, until softened.

3. Meanwhile, add the broth and brandy to the frying pan. Cook over a high heat for 3 minutes, stirring and scraping, until reduced by half. Whisk in the cream and tarragon and simmer for 2-3 minutes, until slightly thickened. Season, then spoon over the chicken packages and leeks. Garnish with tarragon.

Chicken Packages with Tarragon Cream Sauce

Ingredients

4 large skinless, boneless chicken breasts

8 sun-dried tomatoes in oil, drained

8 slices rindless smoked bacon

2 tbsp olive oil

2 cups/1 lb/450g baby leeks

1½ cups/12 fl oz/350ml fresh chicken broth

2 tbsp/30ml brandy

⅔ cup/5½ fl oz/150ml light (single) cream

2 tbsp/30g chopped fresh tarragon, plus extra to garnish

salt and black pepper

Method

1. To make pesto, place basil leaves, parsley, Parmesan or Romano cheese, pine nuts or almonds, garlic, and black pepper to taste in a food processor or blender and process. With machine running, slowly add oil and continue processing to make a smooth paste.

2. Cook pasta in boiling water in a large saucepan following package directions. Drain and divide between serving bowls. Top with pesto, toss to combine, and serve immediately.

Ingredients

1 lb fettuccine or other
pasta of your choice

Basil and Garlic Pesto:

1 large bunch fresh basil

½ bunch fresh parsley, broken into sprigs

Pesto Pasta

½ cup/4oz/125g grated Parmesan or Romano cheese

¼ cup/4oz/125g pine nuts or almonds

2 large cloves of garlic, quartered

freshly ground black pepper

⅓ cup/3½ fl oz/100ml olive oil

45

Method

1. Line six individual pie pans with the dough. Preheat the oven to 200°C/400°F.

Melt butter in a frying pan and cook onions until golden. Divide into six portions

and spread over base of pies.

2. Combine eggs, sour cream, nutmeg, and horseradish. Pour into pie crusts.

Top with cheese and bake for 20 minutes or until firm.

Tip:

If fresh dill is unavailable, substitute 1 tsp/5g dried dill or ¼ tsp/1.25g ground dill.

French Onion Pies

Ingredients

3 sheets puff dough, thawed

6 onions, sliced

4tbsp/2oz/60g butter

3 eggs, beaten

1¾ cups/12fl oz/350ml sour cream

1 tsp/5g ground nutmeg

1½ tsp/7.5g horseradish relish

1½ cups/6oz/175g sharp yellow cheese, grated

Method

1. Cook salmon on a lightly oiled preheated barbecue or under

a broiler. for 3-5 minutes each side or until firm.

2. Combine all the ingredients for the salsa. Serve with the salmon.

Ingredients

4 salmon steaks

Pineapple Salsa:

1 cup/8oz/250g canned crushed pineapple, drained

2 green onions (scallions), chopped

1 fresh red chili pepper, chopped

1 tbsp/15ml lemon juice

2 tbsp/30g chopped fresh mint

Salmon with Pineapple Salsa

Method

1. Cook the gnocchi according to the package instructions. Drain well, then transfer to a shallow flameproof dish.

2. Preheat the broiler to high. Place the pine nut kernels in the broiler pan and toast for 2-3 minutes, stirring from time to time, until golden. Keep an eye on them as they can burn quickly.

3. Meanwhile, put the mascarpone and gorgonzola cheese in a saucepan and warm over very low heat, stirring until melted. Season to taste. Spoon the mixture over the gnocchi, then broil for 2-3 minutes, until bubbling and golden. Scatter the pine nut kernels over the dish and serve.

Gnocchi with Mascarpone and Blue Cheese

Ingredients

14 oz/400g package fresh gnocchi

1 tbsp/15g pine nut kernels

½ cup/4oz/125g mascarpone

1 cup/8oz/250g gorgonzola cheese, crumbled

salt and black pepper

Method

1. Place oil, soy sauce, garlic, and ginger in a bowl and mix to combine. Add chicken and marinate for 15 minutes.

2. Drain chicken, thread onto lightly oiled skewers, and cook under a preheated medium broiler or on a barbecue for 15-20 minutes, or until chicken is cooked.

3. To make sauce, heat oil in a saucepan over a medium heat, add garlic and ginger and cook, stirring, for 2 minutes. Stir in broth, coconut milk, and soy sauce, bring to a simmer, and simmer for 5 minutes.

4. Add peanut butter and simmer for 5 minutes longer.

Just prior to serving, stir in chili sauce. Serve sauce with chicken.

Note: The sauce can be made in advance and stored in a sealed container in the refrigerator for 5-7 days. Reheat over a low heat before serving. If sweet chili sauce is not available mix ordinary chili sauce with a little brown sugar.

Ingredients

1 tbsp/15ml vegetable oil

1 tbsp/15ml soy sauce

1 large clove of garlic, crushed

½ tsp/2.5g finely grated fresh ginger

1lb/500g boneless chicken thigh or breast fillets, skinned and cut into

1in/2.5cm cubes

Quick Chicken Satay

Satay sauce:

1 tsp/5ml vegetable oil

2 large cloves of garlic, crushed

2 tsp/10g finely grated fresh ginger

1 cup/8fl oz/250ml chicken broth

1 cup/8fl oz/250ml coconut milk

1 tbsp/15ml soy sauce

2 tbsp/10g crunchy peanut butter

2 tsp/10ml sweet chili sauce

quick & delicious

Method

1. Peel and slice the avocado and place in a bowl together with the red beets, celery, and apple. Cover and set aside. Preheat the broiler to high and lightly toast the bread for 2–3 minutes each side. Place a slice of Brie cheese on top of each toast, then return them to the broiler. Cook until the cheese is melted and golden.

2. Meanwhile, to make the dressing, place all the ingredients in a small saucepan and bring to the boil, simmer for 2–3 minutes, until warmed through.

3. To serve, divide the salad leaves between four plates, top with the red beet mixture and place a cheese toast on each plate. Drizzle with the warm dressing and serve immediately.

Grilled Brie With Red Beet Salad

Ingredients

1 avocado

1 cup/8oz/250g cooked red beets, drained and chopped

2 celery sticks, sliced

1 red dessert apple, cored and chopped

4 slices white bread

½ cup/4oz/125g brie cheese, quartered

1 cup/4oz/125g mixed salad leaves

Dressing:

3 tbsp/45ml extra virgin olive oil

3 tbsp/45ml cider vinegar

1 clove of garlic, crushed

1 small red onion, minced

1 tbsp/15ml tomato paste

sea salt and freshly ground black pepper

Method

1. To make dressing, place yogurt, coriander, cumin, and chili powder to taste in a bowl and mix to combine. Cover and chill until required.

2. To make patties, place beef, garlic, bread crumbs, egg, tandoori paste, and soy sauce in a bowl and mix to combine. Divide beef mixture into four portions and shape into patties.

3. Heat a little oil in a frying pan over a medium-high heat. Add patties and cook for 4-5 minutes each side or until done.

4. Place a lettuce leaf, some tomato slices, 2 cucumber slices, a patty, and 1 tbsp/15ml dressing on the bottom half of each roll. Cover with the other halves.

Tip

If tandoori paste is not available, use curry paste and add a few drops of red coloring to it before use.

Tandoori patties:

1 lb/500g lean ground beef

2 cloves of garlic, crushed

2 tbsp/30g dried bread crumbs

1 egg

1½ tbsp/20ml tandoori paste

1 tbsp/15ml soy sauce

vegetable oil

Ingredients

4 whole-wheat bread rolls,

split and toasted

4 lettuce leaves

2 tomatoes, sliced

8 slices cucumber

Tandoori Beef Burgers

quick & delicious

Spiced yogurt dressing:

⅓ cup/3 ½oz/100g natural yogurt

1 tbsp/15g chopped fresh coriander

½ tsp/2.5g ground cumin

pinch of chili powder

57

Method

1. First make the salsa. Put the tomatoes in a bowl and cover with boiling water. Leave for 30 seconds, then skin, deseed, and dice. Combine with the pineapple, garlic, chili, oil, lime juice, and coriander. Season to taste and set aside.

2. Preheat the broiler to high. Score the fat around the edge of each steak and rub all over with the thyme sprigs. Brush with honey and broil for 2-3 minutes on each side, until tender and cooked through. Serve with the salsa and lime wedges, garnished with coriander leaves.

Honeyed Ham Steaks with Pineapple Salsa

Salsa

2 tomatoes

1 cup/oz/250g pineapple, cut into ½ in/1cm cubes

1 clove of garlic, crushed

1 red chili pepper, deseeded and chopped

2 tbsp/30ml extra virgin olive oil

juice of ½ lime

2 tbsp/30g chopped fresh coriander (cilantro)

salt and black pepper

Ingredients

4 thick smoked ham steaks, about 8oz/250g each

2 sprigs fresh thyme

1 tbsp/15ml clear honey

lime wedges to serve and fresh coriander (cilantro) to garnish

Method

1. Cook the potatoes in a large saucepan of lightly salted water for 15 minutes or until tender. Meanwhile, mash together half of the butter, the mint, cumin, and a little pepper, then cover and refrigerate. Put the cream and saffron strands in a small pan, gently heat through, then remove from the heat and set aside for 5 minutes to infuse.

2. Preheat the broiler to high. Season the lamb steaks and broil for 4-5 minutes on each side, or until cooked to your liking. Cover with foil and leave to rest for 5 minutes. Meanwhile, drain the potatoes well and mash with a potato masher, then mix in the remaining butter and the saffron cream, and season to taste.

3. Divide the chilled mint butter between the steaks and broil for a few seconds until it melts. Serve the steaks with the saffron mash and any pan juices. Garnish with mint.

Lamb with Mint Butter and Saffron Mash

Ingredients

2 lb/900g large floury potatoes cut into chunks

salt and black pepper

2 tbsp/1 oz/25g butter, softened

2 tbsp/30g chopped fresh mint, plus extra leaves to garnish

½ tsp/1.25g ground cumin

4 tbsp/60ml light (single) cream

pinch of saffron strands

4 lamb leg steaks

Method

1. Place the chicken breasts between two sheets of plastic wrap, and pound with a rolling pin or steak hammer to flatten them slightly. Unwrap and cut into thin diagonal strips. Place in a non-reactive bowl, season, then add the soy sauce, 1 tbsp/15ml oil. and juice squeezed from one of the lemons. Mix well, cover, and refrigerate for 20 minutes.

2. Heat the remaining oil with the butter in a large heavy-based frying pan until foaming. Add half the chicken strips and fry, stirring, over a high heat for 3 minutes or until golden and cooked through. Transfer to a plate and fry the remaining chicken. Add to the plate and set aside.

3. Mix the cornstarch with 1 tbsp of water until smooth. Add the broth to the pan with the cornstarch paste and stir over a high heat for 2 minutes or until smooth and glossy. Stir in the juice from half the remaining lemon, and the sugar. Return the chicken to the pan and heat for 1-2 minutes, until piping hot.
Serve garnished with thin slices of the remaining half lemon and sprigs of flatleaved parsley.

Lemon Chicken Stir-fry

Ingredients

4 skinless boneless chicken breasts

salt and black pepper

1 tbsp/15ml light soy sauce

2 tbsp/30ml olive oil

2 lemons

2 tbsp/1oz/25g butter

2 tsp/10g cornstarch

1¼ cups/10 fl oz/300ml chicken broth

1 tbsp/15g sugar

coarsely grated rind of

fresh flatleaved parsley to garnish

Method

1. Heat 2 tbsp/30ml of the oil in a large heavy-based saucepan, then
add the peppers, garlic, thyme, 2 tbsp/30ml water, and seasoning.
Cook, partially covered, for 20 minutes or until softened and browned,
stirring occasionally.

2. Meanwhile, season the monkfish well, then wrap a slice of Parma ham
around each fillet. Secure the ham with a wetted cocktail stick. Heat the
remaining oil in a large heavy-based frying pan, add the fillets, and fry for
8–10 minutes, turning once, until browned and cooked through.
Cover loosely with foil and set aside.

3. Add the balsamic vinegar to the peppers in the pan and cook for
5 minutes to warm through. Remove the cocktail sticks, then cut the
monkfish into thick slices, and garnish with the fresh basil.
Serve with the peppers and any pan juices.

Ingredients

3 tbsp/45ml extra virgin olive oil

4 large bell peppers red, green, orange, or yellow, deseeded

and thickly sliced

4 cloves of garlic, minced

2 sprigs fresh thyme

salt and black pepper

Monkfish and Parma Ham with Braised Peppers

4 monkfish fillets, about 8oz/250g each

4 slices Parma ham

2 tbsp/30ml balsamic vinegar

chopped fresh basil to garnish

Method

1. Place oil, onion, garlic. and chili in a microwavable dish. Cover and cook on HIGH (100%) for 3 minutes.

2. Stir in beef, satay sauce, coconut milk, and lemon juice. Cover and cook for 5 minutes.

3. Add green beans and red bell pepper, stir, cover, and cook on MEDIUM (50%) for 5 minutes or until vegetables are tender crisp.

Note: For a complete meal, serve with brown or white rice or oriental noodles.

Ingredients

1 tbsp/15ml peanut oil

1 onion, minced

2 cloves of garlic, crushed

1 tsp/5g finely chopped fresh red chili pepper

1 lb/500g rump steak or chuck steak, cut into thin strips

Peanut Beef Curry

1 scant cup/7oz/220g bottled satay stir-fry sauce

½ cup/4fl oz/125ml coconut milk

2 tbsp/30ml lemon juice

1 cup/8oz/250g green beans, halved

1 red bell pepper, thinly sliced

Method

1. Place spinach in a sieve and squeeze to remove as much liquid as possible.

2. Place cream cheese, feta cheese, eggs, zucchini (courgettes), carrot, red bell pepper, spinach, and black pepper to taste in a bowl and mix to combine.

3. Pour egg mixture into a greased 9in/23cm square cake pan, sprinkle with tasty cheese (mature cheddar) and bake for 25 minutes or until set.

Tip

Serve with wholegrain rolls and a salad of mixed lettuces and chopped fresh herbs. Also delicious cold this cheesecake is a tasty addition to any picnic and leftovers are always welcome in brown bag lunches.

Ingredients

3 cups/12oz/375g frozen spinach, thawed

1 cup/8oz/250g cream cheese, softened

½ cup/4oz/125g feta cheese, crumbled

4 eggs, lightly beaten

2 zucchini (courgettes), grated

1 carrot, grated

1 red bell pepper, chopped

freshly ground black pepper

½ cup/2oz/60g grated sharp yellow cheese

Vegetable Cheesecake

Method

1. Place the pumpkin or squash in a steamer or metal colander, covered with foil. Set over a saucepan of simmering water and steam for 5-10 minutes, or until tender but still firm.

2. Meanwhile, bring the broth to the boil in a small saucepan. Mix the arrowroot with the lemon juice until smooth, then stir in the lemon rind and add to the boiling broth. Simmer, stirring constantly, for 1-2 minutes, until sauce thickens and looks glossy. Add ½ cup/4oz/125g of the cheese and simmer for a further 1-2 minutes, until the cheese has melted. Stir in the dill or parsley, season, and mix well.

3. Preheat the broiler to high. Transfer the pumpkin to a flameproof dish, pour the lemon sauce over it, and sprinkle with the reserved cheese. Place under the broiler and broil for 5-8 minutes, until the sauce is bubbling and golden.

Pumpkin with Lemon and Cheese

Ingredients

3 cups/1½ lb/650g pumpkin or squash, peeled, seeded and cut into chunks

1 cup/8fl oz/250ml chicken or vegetable broth

2 tsp/10g arrowroot

½ lemon, rind grated

1 lemon, juice squeezed

1 cup/8oz/250g mature Cheddar cheese, grated

2 tbsp/50g chopped fresh dill or parsley

salt and pepper

Method

1. Preheat oven to 350°F/180°C. Spray 1 4-cup deep muffin pan (holding 1-cup/8oz/250ml) with canola oil spray.

2. Put the ground meat, onion, carrot, pine nuts, herbs, egg, and bread crumbs in a bowl and mix to combine.

3. Divide mixture among the four greased muffin cups and press in firmly. Spread the tops with the tomato sauce and bake for 30 minutes or until cooked through. Each meatloaf will start to come away from the edges of the cup when cooked.

4. Serve hot or cold with whole-grain bread and salad.

Ingredients

canola (rapeseed) oil cooking spray

2 cups/1lb/480g lean ground beef

1 small onion, finely grated

1 small carrot, finely grated

2 tbsp/30g pine nuts, toasted

Mini Beef and Pine Nut Meatloaves

1 tsp/5g mixed dried herbs

1 egg, lightly beaten

1 cup/4oz/125g fresh bread crumbs

2 tbsp/30ml reduced salt tomato sauce

Method

1. Preheat the oven to 450°F/230°C. Toss the sweet potatoes with the garlic, rosemary, and 2 tbsp/50ml the oil. Transfer to a small roasting pan and cook for 20 minutes, stirring halfway through, until softened. Crush the peppercorns, using a pestle and mortar. Brush the salmon fillets with the remaining oil, coat with the crushed peppercorns, and season.

2. Heat a ridged cast-iron grill pan or heavy-based frying pan. Add the salmon fillets, skin-side down, and cook for 4 minutes, then turn and cook for a further 1 minute, until cooked through. Cover with foil and set aside.

3. Spoon the potatoes and any pan juices onto plates and top with the salmon fillets. Drizzle over a little olive oil, and serve garnished with lemon wedges and rosemary.

Ingredients

1½lb/650g sweet potatoes, cut into ½ in/1cm dice

2 cloves of garlic, roughly chopped

1 tbsp/5g chopped fresh rosemary, plus sprigs to garnish

3 tbsp/45ml olive oil

1 tbsp/15g black peppercorns

4 salmon fillets, about 6 oz/175g each

Seared Salmon with Rosemary Sweet Potatoes

salt and black pepper

olive oil and lemon wedges to serve

fresh rosemary to garnish

Method

1. To make the sauce, place the shallots, wine and 5 tbsp/75ml of the vinegar in a saucepan. Boil for 5-10 minutes, until the liquid has reduced to 1 tbsp/15ml. Strain, discard the shallots, then return the reduced liquid to the pan and set aside.

2. Place the fish, side-by-side and skin side down, in a large saucepan. Barely cover with cold water and pour over the remaining vinegar. Slowly bring to a simmer, then cover and remove from the heat and set aside.

3. Place the spinach in a large pan and cook for 3-4 minutes, until wilted. Squeeze out any excess liquid, then season. Heat through the reserved wine liquid, then whisk in the butter to give a creamy sauce. Add the chives and season. Drain the fish thoroughly, arrange on plates with the spinach, then drizzle with the chive butter sauce.

Tip

If smoke haddock is not available, use other smoked fish, such as mackerel or cod.

Smoked Haddock with Chive Butter Sauce

Ingredients

4 pieces smoked haddock fillet with skin, about 6oz/175g each

2 cups/8oz/250g fresh spinach, stalks removed

salt and black pepper

Sauce:

3 shallots, minced

6 tbsp/90ml dry white wine

6 tbsp/90ml white wine vinegar

⅔ cup/5oz/150g unsalted butter, diced

3 tbsp/45g snipped fresh chives

Method

1. Preheat the oven 425°F/220°C. Put 2 large cookie sheets into the oven to heat.

2. Rinse the shrimp, and pat dry with kitchen towels. Heat the oil in a large heavy-based frying pan, add the garlic, shrimp, and squid and stir-fry for 3 minutes, or until the shrimp turn pink and the squid is opaque.

3. Spread the pizza bases with the tomato paste and top with the cooked seafood, anchovies, and mozzarella. Place on the heated cookie sheets and cook for 10-12 minutes, or until the cheese is golden, swapping shelves halfway through. Scatter the arugula (rocket) over the pizzas. If using parmesan shavings, slice them from a block of cheese using a cheese-slice or vegetable peeler and sprinkle over the pizzas.

Ingredients

24 whole raw peeled tiger shrimp, defrosted if frozen

2 tbsp/30ml olive oil

2 cloves of garlic, crushed

12 small prepared squid tubes, cut into rings

2 x 9 in pizza bases

2 tbsp sun-dried tomato paste

16 anchovy fillets in oil, drained and chopped

Seafood and Arugula Pizzas

1¾ cups/14oz/400g shredded mozzarella

½ cup/2oz/50g arugula (rocket)

Parmesan to serve (optional)

Method

1. Preheat the oven to 400°F/200°C. Arrange the peaches, cut-side up,
in a 12x10in/30x25cm ovenproof dish. Sprinkle with the ginger. Boil the reserved
juice in a saucepan for 5 minutes or until reduced by a third. Pour it over the
peaches.

2. In a large bowl, mix together the flour, hazelnuts, sugar, and cinnamon.
Add the butter and rub in with the tips of your fingers until the mixture resembles
fine bread crumbs. Sprinkle over the fruit and bake for 30-35 minutes, until
browned.

Peach and Hazelnut Crumble

Ingredients

1¾ cups14oz/400g canned peach halves
in natural juice, drained reserving
1 cup/8fl oz/250ml of juice
3 pieces stem ginger in syrup,
drained and finely chopped

1 cup/4oz/125g all-purpose (plain) flour
1 cup/4oz/125g toasted chopped hazelnuts
4 tbsp/60g soft light brown sugar
1 tsp/5g ground cinnamon
½ cup/4oz/125g butter, cubed

Method

1. Preheat the broiler to medium. Place the peach halves, cut-side up, in a broiler pan and top each one with a drizzle of honey and a knob of butter, reserving half the butter for frying. Broil for 5-6 minutes, until softened and golden.

2. Meanwhile, whisk together the eggs, sweet white wine, sugar, lemon juice, and cinnamon. Dip the slices of brioche in the egg mixture to coat.

3. Melt the remaining butter in a large frying pan and gently fry the brioche slices for 2-3 minutes on each side, until crisp and golden. Top each slice with 2 peach halves and their juices and a spoonful of crème fraîche or whipped cream.

Sweet Brioche with Broiled Peaches

Ingredients

4 large, ripe peaches, halved and pitted	2 tbsp/50g superfine (caster) sugar
1 tbsp/15ml clear honey	1 tbsp/15ml lemon juice
6 tbsp/3oz/85g unsalted butter	pinch of ground cinnamon
2 medium eggs, lightly beaten	4 slices brioche
2 tbsp/30ml sweet white wine	crème fraîche or whipped cream to serve

Method

1. Cut cake into 2in/5cm squares. Split each square horizontally and set aside.

2. To make filling, place cream and chocolate in a heatproof bowl set over a saucepan of simmering water and heat, stirring, until chocolate melts and mixture is smooth. Remove bowl from pan and set aside to cool. Beat filling until light and fluffy.

3. Spread filling over bottom half of cake squares and top with remaining cake squares.

4. To make the frosting, sift the powdered sugar and cocoa powder together in a bowl, add butter and mix to combine. Stir in enough milk to make a frosting with a smooth coating consistency.

5. Dip cake squares in frosting to coat completely. Roll in coconut and dust with sweetened cocoa powder. Refrigerate until ready to serve.

Tip

Lamingtons are a type of Australian cookie.

Ingredients

1 butter or sponge cake

(about 7x11in/3.5x27.5cm)

2 cups/8oz/250g unsweetened shredded coconut

1 tbsp/15g sweetened cocoa powder, sifted

Chocolate Cream Filling:

1¼ cups/10fl oz/300ml heavy (double) cream

1 cup/8oz/250g dark baking chocolate

chopped

Shaggy Dog Lamingtons

Chocolate Frosting:

2 cups/8oz/250g powdered (icing) sugar

2 tbsp/30g unsweetened cocoa powder

2 tbsp/30g butter, softened

¼ cup/2 fl oz/50ml milk

Method:

1. Paste the raspberries and elderflower cordial until smooth in a food processor or with a hand blender. Blend in the powdered sugar. Spoon 1 tbsp/15g of the mixture into each sundae glass, reserving the remaining paste, and set aside.

2. Whisk the cream until it holds its shape, then gradually fold in the reserved raspberry paste.

3. Spoon the raspberry cream into the glasses and chill in the fridge for 30 minutes. Serve decorated with the extra raspberries and mint and dusted with powdered sugar.

Raspberry and Elderflower Fool

Ingredients

3 cups/1lb 10oz/750g raspberries, defrosted if frozen, plus extra to decorate

4 tbsp/60ml elderflower cordial

4 tbsp/60g powdered (icing) sugar, to taste, plus extra to dust

2 cups/500ml double (heavy) cream

fresh mint to decorate

87

Method

1. Place raisins and brandy in a bowl and set aside to soak for 15 minutes or until raisins soften. Preheat the oven to 350°F/180°C.

2. Place chocolate and butter in a heatproof bowl set over a saucepan of simmering water and heat, stirring constantly, until mixture is smooth. Remove bowl from pan and set aside to cool slightly.

3. Place eggs and brown sugar in a bowl and beat until thick and creamy. Add chocolate mixture, flour, nuts, and raisin mixture and stir to combine.

4. Pour mixture into a greased 8in/20cm square cake pan and bake for 35 minutes, or until firm. Cool brownies in pan. Then cut into squares and dust with superfine sugar and drinking chocolate.

Rum Raisin Nut Brownies

Ingredients

½ cup/4oz/125g raisins

¼ cup/2 fl oz/60ml brandy

½ cup/4oz/125g dark chocolate, chopped

½ cup/4 oz/125g unsalted butter

2 eggs

1 scant cup/7oz/200g brown sugar

1 cup/4 oz/125g all-purpose flour, sifted

1 cup/4oz/125g macadamia or brazil nuts, chopped

4 tbsp/60g superfine (caster) sugar, sifted, for dusting

4 tbsp/60g sweetened cocoa powder, sifted, for dusting

Method

1. Preheat the oven to 450°F/230°C. Place the melted butter, molasses, or sugar, lemon rind and juice and the rum in a 13x9in/28x23cm ovenproof dish and mix well. Add the bananas and toss to coat. Cook for 12-15 minutes, basting frequently, until the bananas have softened.

2. Meanwhile, warm the milk in a small saucepan, but do not let it boil. Beat the egg yolks and sugar until pale and creamy. Beat in the warmed milk, then the flour and cinnamon. Whisk the whites until they form soft peaks, then fold gently into the mixture.

3. Remove the bananas from the oven and reduce the temperature to 400°F/200°C. Pour the batter over the bananas and return the dish to the oven. Bake for 20-25 minutes, until browned and well-risen. Check the pudding is cooked by inserting a skewer in the center; it should come out clean. Allow to cool slightly. The mixture will sink rapidly as it cools, then dust with powdered sugar and serve warm.

Extra-light Banana Clafoutis

Ingredients

6 tbsp/150g butter, melted

3 tbsp/75g molasses or soft dark brown sugar

1 lemon, rind grated, juice squeezed

3 tbsp/45ml rum

2 lb/900g bananas, cut into chunks

1 cup/8fl oz/250ml half-fat milk

4 eggs, separated

3 tbsp/45g sugar

1 cup/4oz/125g all-purpose (plain) flour

1 tsp/5g ground cinnamon

powdered (icing) sugar to dust

Method

1. Preheat the oven to 350°F/180°C. Beat egg yolks with sugar until thick and creamy. Mix in cocoa powder and chocolate. Beat egg whites until soft peaks form. Fold into chocolate mixture. Pour into a greased and lined 9in/25cm springform pan. Bake for 35 minutes. Cool. Garnish with toffee.

2. To make the toffee, melt sugar in a heavy saucepan over high heat. Shake saucepan so that sugar browns evenly. Bring to the boil and cook until golden. Pour onto a sheet of greased foil and leave to set. Break into large pieces.

Ingredients

6 eggs, separated

½ cup/4oz/125g superfine sugar

3tbsp/75g unsweetened cocoa powder, sifted

1 cup/8oz/250g dark chocolate, melted

Flourless Chocolate Cake

Toffee:

½ cup/4oz/125g superfine (caster) sugar

Method

1. Place eggs in a bowl and beat until thick and creamy. Gradually add superfine sugar, beating well after each addition, until mixture is creamy.

2. Combine flour and ground hazelnuts. Fold flour mixture, milk, and butter into egg mixture. Pour mixture into two greased and lined 8in/20cm round cake pans and bake for 25 minutes or until cakes are cooked when tested with a skewer. Turn onto wire racks to cool.

3. To make the filling, place cream and powdered sugar in a bowl and beat until thick. Place caramels in a saucepan and cook, stirring, over a low heat until caramels melt and mixture is smooth. Remove from heat and set aside. Leave to cool slightly.

4. To assemble, split each cake in half horizontally using a serrated cake knife. Place one layer of cake on a serving platter, spread with cream mixture, drizzle with caramel and top with a second layer of sponge. Repeat layers, finishing with a layer of filling, and drizzling with caramel. Decorate top of cake with whole hazelnuts.

Caramel Hazelnut Cake

Ingredients

4 eggs

1 cup/7oz/220g caster sugar

1¼ cups/5oz/155g self-raising flour, sifted

⅓ cup/1½oz/45g ground hazelnuts

½ cup/4fl oz/125ml milk, warmed

½oz/15g butter, melted

2oz/60g whole hazelnuts

Caramel and cream filling:

2 cups/16fl oz/500ml heavy (double) cream

1 tbsp/15g powdered (icing) sugar, sifted

12oz/375g soft caramels

Tip

Caramelized hazelnuts make an elegant garnish for this European-style dessert cake. To make, gently melt a little granulated sugar in a frying pan until it turns a pale golden color. Remove from heat, quickly drop in whole toasted hazelnuts and stir briskly with a wooden spoon until well coated. Cool on an oiled baking sheet or on baking paper.

Index